To _____

From _____

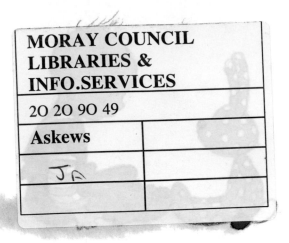
*For my godchildren – Katie, Jamie,
Holly and Amelia – with much love   S.T.*

*For Lorna Burns and Catherine Butler
with my love and thanks   K.S.*

Text copyright © Sarah Toulmin
Illustrations copyright © 2007 Kristina Stephenson
This edition copyright © 2007 Lion Hudson

The moral rights of the author and illustrator
have been asserted

A Lion Children's Book
an imprint of
Lion Hudson plc
Mayfield House, 256 Banbury Road,
Oxford OX2 7DH, England
www.lionhudson.com
ISBN: 978 0 7459 6013 5

First edition 2006
1 3 5 7 9 10 8 6 4 2 0

Acknowledgments
Bible extracts are taken or adapted from the Good News Bible,
published by The Bible Societies/HarperCollins Publishers Ltd, UK
© American Bible Society 1966, 1971, 1976, 1992, used by permission.

A catalogue record for this book is available
from the British Library

Typeset in 20/30 Baskerville MT Schoolbook
Printed and bound in China

Baby Prayers

Sarah Toulmin

Illustrations by Kristina Stephenson

LION
CHILDREN'S

Thank you, God, for all your precious little ones.

Thank you for wide eyes, eager smiles and trusting faces.

Thank you for the miracle gift they are to us. Help us to teach them more about you and your love for them.

Amen

Contents

Wide Awake Time

Every day is a new beginning, and a time to thank God for all that is good and lovely.

Dear God,
Thank you for the joy that can be found in simple things.
Help us to learn and grow together.
Amen

Thank you, God,
for this new day.
Please be with us all,
I pray.

Hello God!
Hello world!
It's me!

Sleep,
Wake

Look,
Sit

Clap, Wave.
That's it.

Sit, Stand,
Walk, Run.
This is good fun.

You and me, me and you.
I like playing peekaboo!

Baby's Busy Day

These prayers are to help you enjoy all the busy but precious times when you and baby are together.

Dear God,

Help me to enjoy taking care of this little child today.

Please give me all the energy

and patience I need.

Amen

Arms won't stop flapping and
legs won't stop wriggling,
As we try to get dressed
I just can't stop giggling.
Fingers in socks, oh no,
what a muddle!
But I know when it's over I'll get
a big cuddle!

Thank you, God, for clothes that keep me snug and warm.

Thank you God for food so yummy,
Makes me strong and fills my tummy.

1, 2, 3, 4, 5,
Thank you God
that I'm alive.

6, 7, 8, 9, 10
Thank you
for this food.
Amen

Anon

Thank you, God, for bathtime,
We all have so much fun.
I splash and splish as I get wet
And so does everyone!

Wash my ears,
Wipe my nose,
Clean my tummy
And tickle my toes.

Holding hands
and walking tall,
this is great –
not scared at all.

On my own
and letting go:
God, please
help me
as I grow.

Out and About

When you go out and about with a baby, you see the world through the eyes of a child again.

Thank you, God, for this amazing world. Help us to discover new wonders every day.

Amen

Dear God, I like to talk to you,
I have so much to say.
I want to learn the words to tell you
all about my day.

Thank you for the golden sun,
Thank you for the sky,
Thank you for the fluffy clouds
that float so very high.

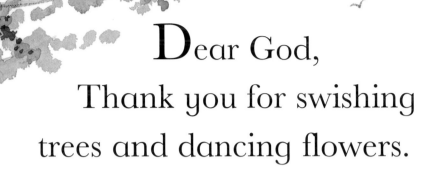

Dear God,
Thank you for swishing
trees and dancing flowers.

Thank you for birds that fly
and fish that swim.

Thank you for spiders that crawl and cats that climb.

Thank you for an amazing world. You must be an amazing God.

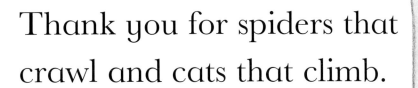

MoOOo

Baaa, bAAa

Quack, quack,
quack

Me-ow

28

Thank you, God, for all
these animals – they
make me happy.
Amen

Shh!

*Eee,
eee, eee*

Thank you, God, that you look after
the big things:

big whales, big bears

and great big elephants.

Thank you, God, that you look after the tiny things:

tiny caterpillars, tiny ants

and teeny, tiny ladybirds.

Thank you, God,
that you look after me.

Dear God,
I like the rain
and big puddles
to splash in.

Wow!

Thank you, God,
for the colours
of the rainbow.

Dear God,
I like the sun
and dancing
with my
shadow.

Thank you, God,
for winter and white
frost;

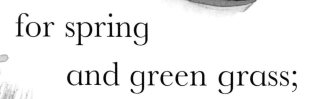

for spring
and green grass;

for summer
and blue sky;

for autumn
and its leaves
of red and orange.

Love

God is Love. As you learn to love your child, pray that you might both learn about God's love.

Dear God,
Thank you for loving us. Help us to love you and one another more.
Amen

Thank you, God, for love.

For hugs and cuddles.
For smiles and kisses.
For giggles and playtime.

For someone who cares when
I'm crying.
For someone who helps me
and feeds me.
For someone who'll always be
near me.

Dear God,
Thank you that you are my friend
and I can always talk to you.
Amen

Dear God,
I am only small
but you are a great big God
and you hold me
and keep me safe.

41

God says this:

I have always loved you.
When you were growing
in your mummy's tummy
I knew all about you.

I am with you all the time.
You are very special to me
and I will always love you.

From Psalm 139, in the Bible

Dear Jesus,
You were born on earth:
God's little baby boy.

Mary
rocked you
to sleep.
Joseph kept
you safe.

People came to visit.
Some brought gifts.

Dear Jesus,
You were born on earth:
a baby like me.

Our Father in heaven,
Your name is amazing.
We want everyone to see that you are king.
We want to do the things that make you happy.
Please give us the things we need.
Forgive us when we do wrong.
Help us forgive others.
Keep us safe, now and always.
Amen

From the prayer that Jesus taught,

in the Bible

What Will I Be?

Whatever your dreams for your baby, pray that they become the person God created them to be.

Dear God,
Thank you that you love us all. Please help me to guide
my child in the way that you want.
Amen

Dear God,

Thank you for the day I was born.

Thank you for my birthday.

Thank you for my life and all the wonderful people who share it with me.

Dear God,
I want to grow up
to explore the world,
to do wonderful things
and enjoy all the blessings
you give me.

Playing,

r u n n i n g,

twirling,

laughing

Thank you, God, for fun and friends.

Dear God,

Thank you for places to explore where I can be brave.

Thank you
for things to
discover so
I can learn.

Thank you for my home where I am safe.

Sleepy Time Blessings

Bedtime is the opportunity to end the day well with a calming prayer and a kiss goodnight.

Dear God,
Thank you for being with us throughout this day.
Please give all in this house
a restful night.
Amen

Dear God,
Why did you make
so many stars
and only one moon?

Did it take a long time to colour in the
sky or did you use a paintbrush?

Ssh: so tired.

Ssh: so sleepy.

Ssh: so cosy.

Ssh: goodnight.

Twinkling stars
Shine down with love,
Moonlight kisses
From above.
Time to rest
Time to sleep,
Heavenly angels
Watch will keep.

Hush little baby
don't you cry;
Angels will sing you
a lullaby.

May God bless you.
May God keep you safe.
May God watch over you always.

Little one, rest your tired head
May angels watch over you in your bed.
May God's love surround you through
the night
and keep you safe till morning light.
Amen.

63

Index